Ordinary Time

Ordinary Time

Poems by

Kathleen Wedl

Susan,
Your friendship is dear
to me —
Love, K.

Cover design by Shay Culligan
Back cover photo by Adair Soderholm

ISBN: 978-1-63980-310-1

Kelsay Books
502 South 1040 East, A-119
American Fork, Utah 84003
Kelsaybooks.com

Acknowledgments

Thank you to the following magazines and journals, where these poems originally appeared, sometimes in earlier forms.

.

82 Review: "Dodging Despair"

Crone Lit Anthology: "Before Calling the Coroner," "My Mother's Hair"

Freshwater Literary Review: "On Advice of the Wedding Planner," "A Full Moon and Its Mischief"

Gyroscope Review: "A History in Brief"

High Shelf Press: "Theology on a Country Road"

League of MN Poets Contest, Mike Finley Humor Award: "The Anti-Muse," "A Fair Trade"

Mason Street: "Wished Away"

Minnesota Voices: "I Am an Orphan"

South 85 Journal: "The One About Eggs"

Thanks first to my husband, Bob Wedl, for his unflagging support; to my mentors, Gretchen Marquette, Alison McGhee, Deborah Keenan, and the alchemists at the Loft Literary Center.

Thank you to my fellow writers: June Blumenson, Elizabeth Weir, Beth Spencer, Sandra Kacher, Cynthia Wold, Diane Pecoraro, and Kathleen Coskran. Thank you to friends and family who stirred encouragement into their love.

Contents

III

There are no ordinary feelings.
Just as there are no ordinary spring days
or kicked-over cans of paint.
—Dean Young

I

Even as I Leave You

inspired by Oliver de la Paz' "At the Time of My Death"

A coyote prowls the suburbs, something wriggling
in its mouth. A hooting owl spies from its perch.

A bicycle, stolen off a porch at three, bears
groceries home for dinner six miles away

& somewhere, a fancy-dress party, a clap of thunder, a train
derailing, its cars shooting wild

into the woods. Somewhere lemurs glide tree to tree
in the moonlight, graceful as goshawks

& always jazz & night ladies' nipples covered
by nothing & suffering & attempts to soothe.

What can I leave you? Autumn leaves, virgin snow?
I leave you stillness and poetry, the *dear*

who have left their tracks on my heart, the eyes
of the owl that see through the dark.

Something You Should Know

you'll find me in the kitchen dancing   I   need   three   squares
nobody is called   square   anymore but that doesn't mean
we're all cool   I entertain my family with tales   of ditzy-
do   if I back into your car a few times   in one day   do I
still get a foot rub?   the accumulation of wealth and power
rub me the wrong way   I would lay me down in the tall
grass with anyone   who makes music   or   Persian
food   once believing in a deity was as easy as licking ice
cream   ice   cream   melts   numbers   don't   lie
something happened to me as a child   I was not believed
sagging skin crepes me out   before my time   when the
dearly departed were laid out in the parlor   mirrors and
windows were hung with black crepe   creepy
wool   gathered   here
touch receptors in my fingers and arms   ache to gather you
deep   within   my   six-foot   perimeter

A History in Brief

I'm from bean fields, shocked wheat, seed caps, canned peaches,
        long johns hanging cardboard stiff on the porch.

I'm from five and dime—dad forcing smiles at indoor chores
        ringing up lady things, paper dolls, candy leeches.

I'm from nuts and bolts, stacked paint cans, pitchforks, mowers,
        guns, china place settings—parents' easy smiles.

I'm from convent school, town dances, ripped lips from braces,
        late night cars purring beneath mounds of snow.

I'm from hospital wards, monitors, bed pans, hands reaching
        to be held, one who made me holy, one who spat in
        my eye.

I'm from rivers of sweet woodruff, chorus of coral bells,
        hydrangeas deigning to bloom and those four giddy
        poppies waving in spring.

The Crib

In my first memory, I'm gripping bars—
chipped ivory paint over dull metal.

Safe, but I want out. My wish is granted
when the baby comes, my new bed a sofa

in the living room where dark shadows
and sounds spook my dreams. A rocker

rocks itself. The hired man lies blocking
the doorway, a rooster on his belly. It pecks

me as I try to cross into the bedroom.
My screams stop only when Dad wakes me,

his soft voice croons, cocoons
like the bars of the crib once did.

The Anti-Muse

Bob says we had a good day in the stock market. Doubt
stands in the corner rolling her eyes. *It's all ether,*
she says, pricking the bubble with her barbed wire chin.

We happily scan maps, plan a drive across Portugal.
See you at the morgue, Doubt says. *On the bright side
it's cheaper to ship home ashes than to book two seats.*

I have us packed and ready to leave at dawn for the annual
family lake reunion, trick the harpy into staying home, but she's
roosting like winged Buddha on the hood, wondering out loud if this
will be the year someone will be decapitated by a drunken boater.

I write a pretty good poem. Doubt twirls a lock of hair round a pointy
finger, says, *That was a jammy tidbit. Here's a hundo you can't do
it again. Anyway, shouldn't you be ironing?*

She hoots when I comfort a sick friend with a promise of prayer,
calls me a flimflam fake, says I could do more with chicken soup.

Mother's Day, I wring every drop of joy from hand-written notes,
flowers, family togetherness. Doubt examines a message that
brought me to tears, tosses it back, says, *Aren't they required to kiss
up today?*

She's speechless when I'm in the spring garden enraptured
among electric blue forget-me-nots, columbine and iris.
Thrilled to shut her up, I tape post-it's around the house—
affirmative words like *peace, confidence, aplomb. Aplomb*
burrows beneath her warty skin. While Doubt scratches,
damned if I don't see my muse swaggering up the block.

Self-Portrait, Wanting

I want lasagna and the pencil skirt
sailing waves and glassy lake
I want spring rain and sun-kissed hours
Portofino and 401k

I want to hoard time for my art
but lavish it on causes
to cook a feast as time stands still
to dream, to think, put life on pause

I'd like another lustful romp
but think I'll turn in early
Scotch and soda, glass of red
then wake free of penalty

I want to see the pyramids
but give nothing to the dictator
to meet my countrymen half-way
just this side of center

Give me ineffable mystery
and anointed truth
velvet and hairshirt
ashes and grave

at ten I was an owlet

facing a murder of crows
      an Argus-eyed nocturnal warrior
           just short of plumage and pluck
               my fate a dangling branch

steadied or stirred   by the god of mellow mouse purr
           or vengeful tempest

I crawled before I flew
my kid sister   guarding me in the dark

                    she
blind to the shadow   insensitive to boney branches
     tracing the backs of our necks
                   she
        of the dimpled   heart-faced owlets
opens wide her wings
      unruffled
        certain of favorable winds

A Fair Trade

You give me Honeycrisp
      I give you prickly pear

You give me spring's first strawberry
      I give it back (you insist)

You give me twigs
      I give you nest

You do the heavy lifting
      I simmer and stir

You give me *Brave New World*
      I give you *Great Expectations*

You give me six spades
      I give you a small slam

You give me mown grass
a tank with gas
      I place daisies at your plate

You give me the palm of your hand
undulating down my naked spine
slick with almond oil
      I give you a sleepy kiss

Your love is a warm slipper on a frosty night
      Let me light the fire

What to See: A Traveler's Guide

We travel better young,
standards less exacting.
A veteran wanderer,
I whip through hotel rooms
with bleach wipes
wishing I had never seen
hidden camera videos
of maids cleaning glasses
with the toilet cloth.

I pull back the mattress pad,
search for bed bugs, stress
over roach eggs, require
hot showers and high
thread count, scan
those never washed
decorative pillows
for sperm count and pubic hair.

Oh, to return with eyes
unjaded, to the room above
that Granada café,
three bucks a night, cockroaches
marching through open suitcases.
We see only the scene beneath
our balcony—children all starch
and white lace, processing
down the alley hand-in-hand,
to the trill of church bells,
inhale the aroma of fresh espresso.

When even that quick glimpse
of the Alsatian kitchen
would not spoil our kuchen,
counters teeming with bunnies
their brown pellets
scattered everywhere.

novelty

she owned a handmade violin
        played only the year   she tried the convent
stopped   when she tried marriage.

she wabbled it on brackets
        to decorate   over the sofa
an unearned trophy   no surprise

it desiccated
        shattered as it fell off the rail
            she gathered the pieces in a grocery bag

        took them to a grizzled violin repair man
he heard her weak confession   as he picked   through the mess
        of maple   spruce   and string   fondled bits of burl

then turned his back
        dumped the remains in the trash

she thought she might retrieve the pieces
save the shards   the filaments   mount them in a shadow box

        a reminder gentle as a hammer

monument to half-measures
how funny would that be

Fade-proof Snapshots

Here's one of The Slap, flash to bang, thought to thwack
leaving this mulish wall of regret and rage, this burrowing welt.

        It was a snarky remark—the cheek of you
        a retort as you sat at the piano, playing it your way.

The mark meant I had to keep you home from a sleep-over.
What possible alternative truth
could explain the cackling red fact of it?

        We can almost hear the piano clear its throat
        as if to say, *Step away, Lady. That's not the way*
        to foster music appreciation.

This is my hand, possessed, like an impulsive punk at the controls.
Hurts you more than it hurts us both.

        And in this one, the way you hide the wild bird of
        your love these forty years later, wear it fleetingly
        on your sleeve, then hood it to hold inside.

Here's me tiptoeing through cinders of shame and apology,
with a letter laying open a need to hold your hand,
hear you tell those wry stories—
        not this one.   The ones that make us laugh.

The Blessing

He lingers in the doorway
clutching in his fist a gift
wrapped in Sunday funnies.
On his way to a children's party,
his face no match for the occasion.

Their eyes meet. His brother,
lying on the living room sofa,
is fevered and pocked—
his chin juts a pedestal for pouty lips.

The party-bound boy's eyes
beg forgiveness.
His brother picks at scabs,
savoring this rare power.

The penitent sighs, turns to leave.
Then from the sofa comes
the blessing—
"Well, where's my kiss, stupid?"

X altation

A third of sex but 2/3 if you don't count the real estate
Bane to poets crafting an abecedarian
Crossroads to heaven or hell
Double boomerang belched by a black hole
Even more with tra
Following ape—the pinnacle
Girder's feel their grip
Hides silent in French waters
I'll be banished with X
Jumping jacks in human form
Khakis are seldom worn by XX
Lizzie Borden likes them
Most students abhor them
Name when you haven't learned your letters
O's pair up for games and kisses
Pose with X for a centerfold
Q = Sharon Olds' poem that inspired X
Roll with it for some fine wrist candy
S added on puts it over the top
T and M preceding make some good grub
Uncover the way out with *it*
V before it chaps my hide
Without it our neighbor to the south would be Mico
With act, X is right on the money
X and Pat live abroad
Yaks yikes yolks make cracking good X
Zap the corner of your screen with X to end this poem

On Advice of the Wedding Planner

They jump over brooms to the rhythm of drums.
Bound by red strings, they drink wine and honey
from a two-handled cup—nine sips.

Church records are consulted, for to be conceived
of the same mother is an abomination. In her pocket
a sprinkle of salt, a chunk of bread. His brother showers

their heads with anemone petals while friends gird them
in a heart-shaped ring. With a phallus-shaped summer squash
they whack a pinata, releasing doves—a sign of fertility.

She wears a crown of rosemary leaves, a white hood
meant to hide a woman's horns. A fat pig is drawn,
quartered, roasted—another sign of something—

incantations and execrations against evil. He circles
her finger with a ring of iron. Ten witness's sign.
For this day alone they are stars in a galaxy yet unborn.

Prophecy

In time you will find your rigor mortised love
too late for rescue   too soon   too soon

In time you will pack   or others will pack you
off to a place for those whose choices have gone fallow
you will follow others down long hallways
play bingo   exercise sitting down

In time your drinks will go from something cool and fizzy
to something thickened   akin to Castor Oil
Tennis is a memory   beanbag toss a thing

In time you will forfeit the password to your holdings
your car keys   your wedding ring   You will smile
for your caregivers   your only currency to buy benevolence

In time you will learn to drop pieces
of yourself   like rose petals before a bride
taking measured steps toward the unknown

What A Psych Nurse Remembers
While Driving Home at Midnight

Silas steals glances at the security doors, gauging his chances, feigns indifference. They found him in his basement, kicking aside the chair that supported him, tightening the noose. Landing in lock-up, a wild-eyed wolf, he stalked the exits. How quickly he's learned the game that will buy his freedom.

Blood-tinged water like pink lemonade swirls down the drain. A teen-age beauty has fashioned a stylet from her barrette and probed her sutures lacing older wounds. She allows gauze to seal the leak. *I felt dirty. It's no big deal. Gee, that's a cool watch. Want to play cards?*

Tank you, little girl, murmurs the Norwegian farmer who thinks I am his granddaughter come to help him with his evening ablutions. He will settle on the toilet only after he removes every stitch from his withered body like a lover with nothing but time. Only his once red socks remain. No use fretting about getting the nine o'clock meds out, we will be here together for a while.

A young mother is improving, but still not allowed to the bathroom unescorted. She is a person you would instantly like and trust to watch your children. Still visible on her velvety belly are words she carved in caps: *SLUT, WHORE, BITCH.*

Gone to a place deep inside, someone's grandmother watches from her belted geri-chair. No use for guile. No use for the spoon carrying soup toward her pursed lips. Only touch breaks through. Her arms no longer pull away. Her hand reaches to warm our thin, thin bond.

II

Portrait in Blues

Loneliness idles, like cars at the intersection of other people's lives.

Loneliness is the barren, arid field of a teen-ager's Sunday afternoon.

A lonely woman who is my mother, waves from the window as I back away.

Lost love is a rose-colored lonely.

In a game of rock/paper/scissors loneliness crushes/covers up/cuts through soul and sinew.

Loneliness is alone time without solace.

The linens of lonely lie unwashed, its dirty dishes stacked on the kitchen floor.

Loneliness' pain is exquisite when faced in a crowded room.

I saw loneliness lying in a hospital bed, able to move only his eyes.

In a game of charades, loneliness *sounds like* hunger growling.

Love and solitude can be balm or beastie, sometimes both.

Loneliness, like any wound, heals from inside out.

Viewed from loneliness, a rocky precipice looks like relief.

Loneliness as poem = erasure.

Mary's Final Tour

With her daughters sprawled on her bed
assembled to divide and cast lots,

Mary bewilders through the rooms,
taking mental snapshots—a tourist

who knows this is her last cruise.
She pats the porcelain cat, flicks

through hangers of suits and frou-frou,
mugs to the girls with ropes of glass beads.

Out her kitchen window she notices the first
pair of purple martins to set up housekeeping

in the martin house her Honey built.
Dammit, where were you last year?

Embers

their marriage was a controlled burn
until the last chick fledged
the fuel began to pile up before their wedding
how do you bike into the woods on a Vail
engagement trip and bike out barely
speaking but second guessing creates
less zhuzh than wedding plans and their
therapist was invited   Christmas intoxicated
with its scent of pine Joni Mitchell's *River*
looping with Vince Girardi before the first
candle burned down the tricksy babies bewitched
the way they do with their velvet allure
then one couldn't breathe another screamed
with night terrors their games needed coaches
homework filled the evenings lace itched
flannel soothed sparks sizzled into good night
from the outside their union was a sigh
all ease and charm no one heard the crackle
saw the smoke billows wafting from Grove Street
the lingering scent lonelier than imagined

Wished Away

I wish for the days I wished
my teen granddaughters wouldn't sprawl
across my silken bed in street clothes
their pollen infested ripped shorts
and indoor/outdoor socks
defiling my anti-allergy refuge
reveling in their secrets and embarrassments
trying their bravado on each other
like leather bustiers. Where was the sage
warning me to be careful
what I wished for, those long afternoons
all breathable air saturated with happy
chittering and chortling. They're gone.
My satin comforter smooth, fresh
as the first chill of September.

Today I'll gather apples as the air
turns crisp, something to put up for winter.
Think how the jewels will glisten under glass.

Self Portrait, Agitating the Stew

Leave a teen-age girl   in charge of the stew
and be prepared for surprise   a smoosh of cream
or torch of habanero   rabbit's foot or cloven hoof
She knows how to brew   something pleasing to each
palate   but then   out of the red-tailed universe
comes the urge   to toss in eye of newt
She doesn't stop   at a little   when a lot
could pickle the pudding   At first she clings
close to the recipe   measuring each provision
against what is written   but then spins out   roars
down Highway 75 at 100 per   with a carload of girls
screaming for her to stop   Why does she not
Her smoke alarm goes off   every time a boy steams
Fire ensues   she stinks up the place   She burns
she learns   returns to the book   tries more
complex concoctions   In time she's free-styling
words well-seasoned   at a rolling boil.

Dis-integration

It's not working, they say
like marriage is a machine
whose guide shaft
was improperly mounted
no positraction
parts never meshed
all attempts to weld
leave a metallic taste
no amount of lubricant
restores torque
finally a faulty sensor
blows the pressure gauge

they will disassemble
lay out the parts
pick through and divide
the children
listed under moving parts
will move
between them
as each ex finds the whirr
the buzz
the missing varoom

News of the Day

Death toll
in Haiti soars as
forecast warns flooding—

This is
manifestly not
Saigon. Should I call

for the
police or the Ta-
liban? Hang in there.

They need
everything. We are
trying. Thick mud filled

houses
in the village—as
the data comes in

heinous
and disturbing—does
anyone need help?

The flood
is the heaviest
we have ever seen.

Listen
we have to pull to-
gether. Extreme rough

weather
relentless. Now we
only have Jesus.

They tied
our hands from behind
and sold the country.

Dodging Despair

Back on the bus after touring Ephesus
I sink into my own thoughts
when I spot a dazed, draggled man
in faded tunic and loose pants
weave among the stuttering spaces
between cars, buses, and cycles—
a dreamy dervish with no clear
focus until he locks eyes on a fast
approaching car, then leaps
into the windshield
as if he divined this driver
to embrace into the next world.

Glass shatters, tires skid, screams.
Our guide orders, *Keep moving.*
Drive around it.
Someone asks, *Why would he do that?*
He was a drunk, decides the guide.
Just a drunk.

But I know him.
He's my patient curled on the closet
floor, spasming sobs after a helicopter
landed on the hospital roof—his ears
hearing only the blades of war.
He's the man whose shoes never matched
the occasion, who never found the right fork.
The one whose demons grew up with him,
wore his pajamas, wouldn't shut the fuck up.

He's the boy who never said why.

Six Finches

perched on rosy clusters
of Eastern Redbud flash yellow vests,
sweetening my morning tea. Nature's
cathedral—a reason to believe?
I've half a mind to lean
into science, this glory a cosmic accident,
cataclysm of energy and zircon
matter whirling willy nilly through billions
of years and iterations.

My mind's other half was etched
by sisters at St. Michael's, inscribing
in me the doctrine of catechism.
Who made you? God made me?
A skeptic does not roll over easily
but resists, trying on beliefs for a better fit.
It may take more than one lifetime
to weigh Catechism against cataclysm.

Telling

A girl sees her uncle jerk his thumb,
side-eye her father to follow,
screen door blink open and shut.
She steals out another door,
toward the garage where she hears the *tchzz*
of beer caps easing open, sees cigarette
smoke curl toward the corner
where she casts a small shadow.

Funny, she thinks, that no laughter joins
the beer, the cigarettes, the garage huddle.
Voices are hushed, Uncle's words grim—
Collapsed in the church basement
Nothing they could do
Don't tell the women till after dinner

The girl cradles the captive bird
of her thrumming heart, flies to the kitchen
where the women dance their kitchen jig.
Her mother readies the roast, Grandma whips
potatoes, Aunt Katie moves her fluted pies
to the sideboard, and all gabble in bits of English
here, German there. She is breathless, her eyes level
with bellies and knives, but she is not deterred.

Two hours later the girl wanders ghostly
rooms, whose breath reeks of tears
and congealing gravy. The serving forks lie
in wait like two sisters posing. She thinks
of her cousin, Mary, now motherless, while
her own mother is in the next room—alive.
She wonders how mortal the sin of gratitude.

Exhale

When kitchen curtains sheer
the pink-orange flame of sunrise,
I swim where I sit in still waters

A swan preening, the oil of breath
bathes every cell, smooths my ornery feathers,
allows me to abide a crone's flesh and bone.

Theology Lesson on a Country Road

Can I bring my bike?
is my only worry
in the midst of a brief
lesson on the afterlife.
My parents in the front seat
glance at each other,
not wanting to lie
but loathe to discourage
my pursuit of heaven.
Oh, look at the rainbow!
my mother diverts.
I gaze heavenward,
the uninterrupted blue sky—
no rain, no rainbow,
no answer, no bike,
only a crow perched on a creosote pole
meeting me eye for eye.

$$D = P + L \div X$$

after Gretchen Marquette's poem, "S=k. log W"

D=divorce.

Together they	swear:	happy?
pay the bag piper	*I do (n't)*	arts and flowers
for this fantasy	buttoned lips	often work
what the ears hear:	snipes	years of counseling
good actors	in retrograde	missing ingredients
what they can't give:	love/in love	vinegar and oil
mourning mass	*this is my body*	in need of
standing	by her side	half-life
life is just?	a bowl of	salvation salad
too much	alcohol	results in
stinkin thinkin	*Alexa, play me*	lonely x 2
in the garden	refuge from	stress=pain
love/in love	unslept nights	groans
empty	nest	prickly hush
still time to	do over	divide
tally assets	take off	dead parts
swallow hard	listen to what	kids need
their rooms	they knew	too much
unhomed	where	to put the dog down
family +	friends ÷	lawyers =
full problem jar	a new beginning	forever

Died Suddenly

the obituaries begin—
with youthful photos
often boys
always with   *hearts*
soft   tender
absorbent hearts
lacking
serenity's fire wall
This boy night-sweats
futility
sees ravens
where robins roost
finds the kiss of concrete
at dawn's first light
floating toward earth
with a note and the moon
in his hands

Because Who Doesn't Write Sonnets About Pain?

The disks in Annie's back gnaw on her nerves.
Their pointy teeth grind granting no reprieve.
I send my love like it's a balm deserved
but these are times of monitored relief.

Four times her surgeon cuts. Still four times four
her score of pain and now what doc prescribes
slurred oxy for a woman near four score?
To hope for panacea is a lie—

no then, no now not scarred by pain's presence.
Her surgeon, like a priest, takes her aside,
For sins not hers, imposes cruel penance:
You'll feel along your back the stab of knives.

Fear not—in truth, no wound—no blood will flow.
Unless you tell them, no one else will know.

The Visit

Snow dances aglitter—weightless flakes,
    heavy with remembrance.
Her door is ajar as we approach.
    Bob grabs a shovel from the stoop.

    I lie sprawled on the living room floor.
        Light snow falls, so light it breaks my heart.
    Outside I hear voices, the steady scrape
        of shovel on walk, erasing damning footprints,

The boys and I carry food and gifts
    from Friends of the Elderly. These visits
part of our Christmas Eve tradition.
    I call her name as we steal in,

    They walk in without ringing. A family—volunteers
        bringing my Christmas dinner and gifts.
    He must have left the door wide open.
        The woman walks past, calling my name.

I call, even as I see the body,
    telling my nurse self that what I see
is a resuscitation dummy placed here as a joke.
    I walk into the kitchen, still calling.

    It must be too much, the shock of seeing
        my naked body, a rusty pool of blood haloing
    my crushed head, black welts where he kept striking
        after the heft of the brass lamp took me down.

My sons face reality
　　　　there on the floor,
her naked stillness, blood-matted head,
　　　　a shattered lamp the guilty bludgeon.

　　　　The man finds a robe to cover me.
　　　　　　　The boys search for the overturned phone
　　　　while she checks for a pulse,
　　　　　　long gone.

We do everything wrong, contaminating
　　　　the murder scene with our well-meaning prints
before we surrender and wait
　　　　in the crushing winter hush.

Throw-Away Line

A husk of last light catches the tower watching a lone
tugboat on blue water. Some blatherskite bothers our peace,
bleating nonsense to her captive audience. Who said,
"Silence is a fence around wisdom?" A girl cycles by
trailing billows of red scarf. The clouds begin to mizzle,
shroud the scene in gray. Gray brings mullygrubs of gloom.
Gray of taconite, gray of dove crapping on the balcony.
Mother used to stare out the window on a gray day
and mewl at the gloom. Her tone-deaf daughter would
chirp, *Well, turn around.* The blue, the tugboat, the girl lost
in fog—only a matted red tangle at her neck someone
might mistake for blood. Turn around.

III

Bounty

As I like to imagine it, I grew up under
the spell of his muse, in the same town
as the great poet.
He ran with my sister's crowd.
His father and mine maligned
good-for-nothings—
like the day Bly came to town
with a dead fox in his trunk, hard up
and hoping to collect bounty. He wore
sweat rings on his shirt, his hair a nest,
and my father standing in his shop window
shook his head, his own schooling
cut short for work, and look what comes
of too much dreaming.

Praise

for letting me warm my nose in your eye socket
      my toes in your crotch
for the nightly foot rubs I never request

for the times you make me sit still for the retelling
      of your latest dream
stop to lock lips—drop the dishtowel

for the way you cut a thick pork chop
      give me the half with the bone because
you love how I savor it

      Does your God rule the tides
      the secret murmers
      beneath the forest floor
      the trajectory of comets—

if I hadn't gone to the college bonfire
if the wind wasn't blowing smoke in your eyes
causing you to abandon the bombshell for me

if the hand of God hadn't dropped
my roasted wienie into your beer
to the tune of *Maybellene*

After the Last Dance

Here's me then,
head under a turquoise cone,
saving me from a day
air drying in bristle rollers.
My dress hangs
in the dining room
after a second steaming
by Mom, the wrinkle warrior.

With my friends
I'd flipped through racks
of prom frocks
at Amy-Ann Dress Shop,
rows of netting fluff and puff
in confectionary colors.
On rare fair days in May
I basked on the porch roof
slathered in baby oil and iodine
to attract maximum UV rays,
deprived myself of ice cream
to fit the size 9
minty green bouffant.

With my date waiting
at the bottom of the stairs
I descended, the dress
brushing both walls
like a crinolined umbrella.
He looked up and said only, *Wow,*
which I took to mean
I looked amazing
while in fact he could no doubt
see Russia from there.

Desire to be desired dogs me
Even to the years
when a better person's yearning
settles on milk weed for monarchs,
habitats for the unhomed, children
with bountiful tables.
Enough with fancies
of a Zoomable face,
tight skin, plump lips
scales of vanity.

Bring me words
lush and succulent.
Bring them before all roads
leading to imagination
are sludged and sealed.
Bring them not full-on
but side-eyed sneaky.
Drop them on the stoop
in a beribboned box
like a bracelet bouquet
from that first love.

The One About Eggs

Spring is dead to me. Around the time heart-shaped
leaves emerge on my Eastern Redbud biting gnats like
dark animus descend and swarm. The mother suckers travel
40 miles to sup my neck for the blood meal they need
to produce 400 eggs, and so it Do Si Do's. The buggers gift?
Itchy red welts. I know what you're thinking, they're just doing
their job, and don't we suck great quantities of milk from almonds?
Good God, and didn't we just gas 60,000 hens because restaurants
closed for Covid and lo and behold, no one could remember how
to cook an egg? Now the chicks are in hen heaven, flashing A's
in comportment, martyred for doing as they were told, *pump out
eggs for The Man.* Praise for hens. When a blizzard stalls my
parents in a one-bible motel the night before I was to host
my first Thanksgiving, I sob real tears, dream I phone their room,
yelling, *That's the last fucking turkey I'm dressing,* all about my
disappointment, no matter they're stranded for three days in a
dreary box, no TV, no restaurant, not even a deck of cards. More
tears for the pies, Mom's warm, flakey pumpkin pies they're
forced to eat with their hands. We donate the turkey to Loaves and
Fishes. What does this have to do with eggs? Thanksgiving. We
eat them scrambled.

Circus Novicius

Cherish, from carus, latin for costly
as in be careful of what you hold,

Dear. Rain, bleak and oblique riffs
off the roof of this circus tent

hails spit balls from the Master telling me—
what exactly?   I'm contorting

as fast as I can   bending on command
trusting/not trusting my spine won't snap.

Once I had a crush on a crested ibis
of a man, resplendent, gracile,

a man of troubling repute, and me like macular
degeneration, unable to see deceit straight on.

If time is measured by the loves
of your life, what is time divided by loss?

Save yourself. Secure the silk like an aerial artist
hand over hand, leg over leg, pull and climb.

Sex After Seventy

We play gin rummy.
With each shuffle the king pats
The queen on the rump.

My Mother's Hair

My hair are so terrible,
she complains, using the plural
as if each strand hangs guilty.

Her hairdo is eighty years strong
judging from photos of these finger
waves set into the top of her head, fluted

like pie crust. She keeps a rake behind the door
to smooth vacuum cleaner tracks, ironing board
ready should a wrinkle arise. Beware the bathroom

where Aqua Net hairspray lingers, laminates tonsils—
the spray can a lasso she twirls, rounding up loose ends,
a refinement rodeo.

Picnic

A hilltop in France
      Flies swarm a horse's muzzle
His tail swats in vain

Wine from a tipped glass
      Pools in the dip of your neck
A tempting vessel

Winter

we warm each other
your hand on my breast

mine on your remnants
we are two parts vapor

of loose-fire love
rush of rain stick

sold-out blockbuster
leaping lemurs love

I say aren't we lucky
we had that lasting torrent

you sigh like a superhero
with sagging tights

the weatherman predicts
a frontal depression

so sleep, my darling
the dude with the front end

loader will plow
the snow.

A Full Moon and Its Mischief

cheetahs need the moon
  to illuminate their hunt
lions too & night blooming
  cacti need its light to romance bats
& tides time mating rites

  of grunions lunging to shore
dung beetles orient
  to polarized moonlight
& zooplankton's biological clock
  sets to the light of the moon

tonight when you find your way
  in the dark—as you circle my waist
& hope silvers your eyes
  is it luna with her vast to do list
aiming her torch our way

Before Calling the Coroner

With my skin still clinging, dress me in silk,
    anoint my lips with scotch.

Parade me with a jazz band, costumed children,
    pigs in tutus, family clowns.

Chop me up and place me on a mountain top.
    Let the vultures feast.

Burn me inside the belly of a bull
    as the dragon stands witness.

Bury me in a hollowed-out tree trunk
    or beneath the kitchen table.

Exhume my body later, spray it with wine
    and let the band play.

Dance my essence slow and sexy.
    Send me off with the song of laughter.

If a coffin it must be, make it a Lamborghini
    or a warm mixed-berry pie.

I Am an Orphan

of sunbaked faces, sandpaper hands,
the slick of blanched tomato skins, sweat pouring
off kitchen women filling Mason jars—

of horseflies, locusts,
grasshoppers, gophers, meadowlarks, bobolinks,
gregarious dickcissels nesting in sedges.

I am an orphan of burn piles, cow dung, pond scum,
chicken shit and apple blossoms—the soft waft
of spring breeze, bite of icy rain after a thaw—

of affinity for dirt, heft of shovel, tingle
of physical strain, eyes that scan the land
for signs of life and death.

I am an orphan of the prairie—
of undulating ochre wheat fields under
cobalt skies over windbreaks of oak.

low maintenance

hers are barefoot desires

grounded in sand and brambles

she harkens to whispers from backyard pines

covets a breeze to snap the dew point

her wants are pret-a-porter—

you will see her coming and going

a dress well-seasoned

few must-haves make the cut

clean sheets

a song

forever friends

fresh berries in her breakfast bowl

a bud of verse becoming

About the Author

Kathleen Wedl's poetry has been recognized in contests and journals. In 2020 she was chosen to participate in a year-long mentorship at the Loft Literary Center in Minneapolis, which happened to coincide with a pandemic. Hence, poetry happens. During her 50 years as a nurse specializing in behavioral health, writing was a conduit between herself and her world, as her fifty plus published opinion page letters bear out. When not reading, writing, or dabbling with paint, you may find her in the kitchen stirring up a feast for friends and family.